ABOUT THE BOOK

Born on a Texas ranch in 1860, Bill Pickett was a black cowboy who became a legendary rodeo star, touring America and England in Colonel Zack's famous 101 Wild West Show. Bill introduced the art of bulldogging to spellbound audiences and traded jokes and pranks with his fellow performer Will Rogers. This biography of an extraordinary figure from our nation's history captures the flavor of the Old West and shows that Bill Pickett was more than an exuberant entertainer—he was also a brave and much-loved man.

a Let Me Read book

Illustrated by

Lorinda Bryan Cauley

BILL PICKETT

First Black Rodeo Star

SIBYL HANCOCK

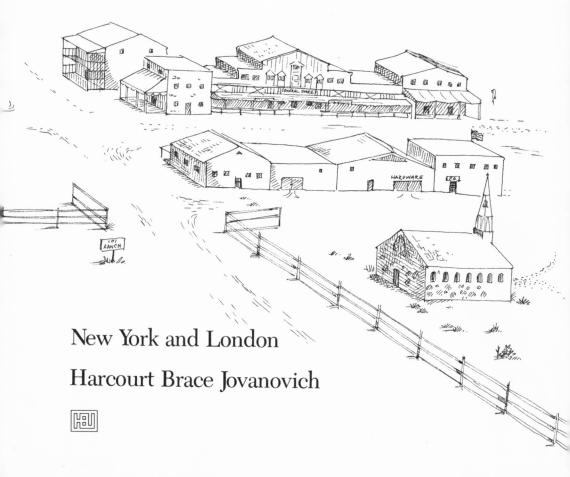

New York and London

Harcourt Brace Jovanovich

Printed in the United States of America

First edition

B C D E F G H I J K

Library of Congress Cataloging in Publication Data

Hancock, Sibyl.
    Bill Pickett: first black rodeo star.

    (A Let me read book)
    SUMMARY: A biography of the black Texan who intro-
duced bulldogging to rodeos.
    1. Pickett, Bill, 1860 (ca.)-1932—Juvenile litera-
ture.   2. Cowboys—Texas—Biography—Juvenile literature.
[1. Pickett, Bill, 1860 (ca.)—1932.   2. Cowboys.
3. Afro-Americans—Biography]   I. Cauley, Lorinda Bryan.
GV1833.6.P5H36   791.8 [B] [92]   76-41741
ISBN 0-15-207392-2
ISBN 0-15-207393-0 pbk.

For Diane, Britt, *and* Eugene

1

Early one morning before the sun came up, Bill Pickett tiptoed out of the back door of his house. His mother and father and little brother were still asleep. Bill was not sleepy. He was worried about a little colt.

Hurrying across the field, he let himself into the barn. The colt was lying in a bed of soft hay. Bill touched the colt. It did not feel hot any more.

"Little horse, here is some water," Bill said.

He smiled when it drank every drop.

"That's good," he said. "You're going to get well now."

Bill could hardly wait to tell his family the good news. He had helped take care of the colt for days. He felt proud. This was not the first time he had taken care of a sick animal. Everyone said that even though he was only a boy, he was good with animals.

Bill Pickett was born in 1860 on a ranch
near Taylor, Texas. Bill's father worked on
the ranch. He was one of many black
cowboys in the West.

Bill's father liked being a cowboy. He
knew how to handle horses and cattle and
how to get along with people.

The ranch was big. Bill always had a lot of
room to run and play. He worked too. He
helped his mother hoe and weed the
garden behind their small house.

One day when his chores were finished, Bill and his little brother ran over to the corral to watch their father and the other cowboys riding wild horses. The corral was a large pen enclosed by a circle of wooden fence.

"Hurray!" Bill shouted. "Look at that horse trying to throw Pa off its back! That's what I want to do some day."

"Not me," his brother said. "You couldn't catch me on a bucking horse."

"Well, I'm going to learn how to ride bucking horses until they're broken," Bill said. "They will be as tame as lambs when I get through."

Bill didn't change his mind about wanting to work on a ranch. When he was about fifteen, he began to ride with the cowboys as they herded cattle. It took many weeks to drive cattle from the ranches to the towns, where they were sold.

After his first trail ride, Bill came home dusty and tired.

"How do you like being a cowboy?" his mother asked him.

"I like it fine," Bill said. "But it's sure not as easy as I thought. Sometimes it rained, and I got all wet. Then other times the wind blew dust so thick I could hardly see."

"Were there any snakes?" she asked.

"Oh, yes," he said. "Big rattlesnakes! And at night when we were sleeping, I could hear coyotes howling."

As he grew older, Bill found jobs that took him away from home. He wandered across southern Texas and into Mexico. For a while he worked on ranches as far away as South America.

He drove cattle through valleys and over hills. He helped men brand or burn a mark into the hides of their cattle. Each ranch had its own brand, so it was easy to know where the cattle belonged.

Bill became skilled at roping calves that
strayed from their mothers. And once he
had to use his gun to kill a mountain lion
that was ready to jump on him. He was
quick with a gun and nearly always hit his
target.

After a time Bill grew tired of drifting from town to town and country to country. He never had a chance to make many friends, and he was lonely. He wanted to settle down in one place and stay. Bill came back to Texas.

One day when he was herding cattle into a corral, Bill saw a tall man watching him. "I like the way you handle a horse," the man said. "My name is Colonel Zack Miller."

"I'm Bill Pickett," Bill said, shaking Colonel Zack's hand.

"I own the 101 Ranch in Oklahoma," Colonel Zack said. "How would you like to work for me?"

"I'd be pleased to work at your ranch," Bill said.

2

Bill had been a cowboy for a long time when he moved to the 101 Ranch. He had seen many ranches, but never one as huge as the 101. Colonel Zack and his brothers had turned the 101 into a regular little town. There was a post office, a school, and a general store. There were even churches, drugstores, and gas stations. The 101 Ranch was famous. People came from all over the country to visit it. Bill felt at home on the 101 Ranch. He soon made friends with the other cowboys.

One of his best friends was named
Ted. For the first time in many years,
he was not lonely.
Ted and Bill were working with some
horses one day when they heard a colt
scream with pain.
Bill quickly found the little horse.
"What is the matter with him?" Ted
asked.
"He's got a big splinter in his chest," Bill
said. "I'll have to get it out."
"Let me help," Ted said.
Ted held the little horse still while Bill
removed the splinter.
"It's going to be a long time before this
colt will be well," Bill said.
For weeks Bill nursed the colt back to
health.

One day the colt seemed almost well.
"Come on, fellow, walk to me," Bill
whispered.
The colt tried to stand, and his legs
wobbled and spread apart.
Bill laughed. "I think your name should be
Spradley!"
Bill visited Spradley every day and always
had a lump of sugar for him to eat. As the
colt grew older, Bill often took him into
wide fields and let him run and kick.
Spradley was becoming a strong and
beautiful horse.

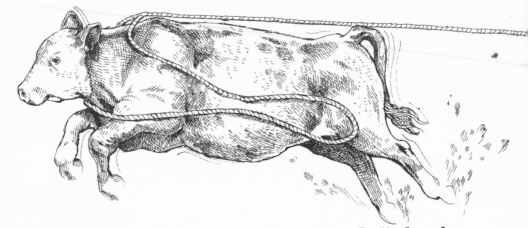

"Spradley looks great," Ted said. "Thanks to Bill's care."

"He sure does," Colonel Zack agreed. He motioned for Bill to come out of the corral. "Well, Bill, how would you like to have Spradley for your own horse?" Colonel Zack asked.

"My own horse?" Bill asked. "I can't believe it. Thank you, Colonel Zack."

"Did you hear that, Ted?" Bill said. "Spradley's *mine*."

Ted smiled. "I heard."

Bill had never been happier. He dearly
loved Spradley. Bill taught him how to
ride beside cattle and how to avoid
their sharp horns. When Bill roped a calf,
Spradley learned to back away so that the
rope would be tight and the calf could not
escape.

When Spradley was grown, he was a very good cowpony. He knew just how to help Bill herd the cattle.

One hot summer day Bill rode after a steer that had broken loose from the herd. He tried again and again to rope it, but he always missed.

"Come on, Spradley, let's get him," Bill said.

Spradley galloped close to the steer, and Bill leaped out of his saddle. He grabbed the old steer's horns with both hands and twisted its head sideways. The steer rolled over on the ground.

Colonel Zack watched and shouted to the men nearby. "Come here! See what Bill did! He threw that steer just like a bulldog does!"

Everyone knew that a bulldog barked and snapped at stubborn cattle. If that did not work, the dog would bite the steer's nose and pull the animal down. But no one had ever seen a man throw a steer using only his hands.

"Do it again," Colonel Zack asked.

Bill grinned. "I sure will," he said.

And he quickly bulldogged another steer.

"You've got to teach me how to do that," Ted told him.

"Me, too," another cowboy said.

Soon all the cowboys wanted to learn how to wrestle a steer to the ground. But not many of them could do it. Only very strong and brave men could bulldog cattle.

It was not long before cowboys from nearby ranches came to the 101 Ranch to see who could bulldog a steer the quickest. The winner went home with a pocketful of money.

"You and Spradley really started something," Ted said. He leaned against the corral gate.

"I guess we did," Bill said. "I've never had so much money to spend."

3

One day Colonel Zack walked over to Bill and said, "More and more people are visiting the 101 Ranch to watch you fellows perform," he said. "I think I'm going to start giving a Wild West Show. I'll make it the best rodeo anyone ever saw. We can have elephants, camels, and buffalo. Maybe even some mules and long-horned steers and bears. Would you do your bulldogging act?"

"That would be fun," Bill said. "Can I use Spradley?"

"Sure," Colonel Zack said.

"I don't believe any rodeo has ever had a bulldogger," Ted said. "Bill will be the first."

When the rodeo opened, there were many cowboys in it besides Bill. Another of Bill's good friends, Will Rogers, was in the show. Will could do rope tricks better than just about anyone else. And he told jokes that made people laugh.

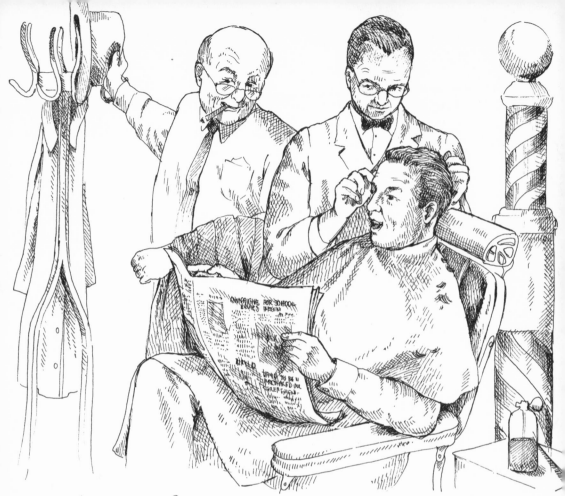

A group of newspapermen came to the 101
Ranch to see the Wild West Show. When
Bill bulldogged a steer, the crowd clapped
and cheered him. His name was printed in
newspapers all over the country.

Being in a rodeo was dangerous. Cowboys took great chances when they worked with wild horses and cattle. The people watching the Wild West Show were frightened but excited by the danger. Spradley traveled everywhere with Bill.

The 101 rodeo went to Madison Square
Garden in New York City. Bill rode
Spradley into the arena after a steer, and
Will Rogers rode nearby.

The steer suddenly jumped over a gate and landed right in the crowd. Nobody was hurt, but the people were scared.

"Hey, Spradley," Bill shouted. "Let's get that steer!"

"I'm right behind you, Bill!" Will Rogers yelled.

Bill leaped from Spradley and grabbed the steer's horns.

"I've got you now, old critter," Bill said. Will Rogers roped the animal's hind legs. He pulled the steer down into the arena with Bill holding onto the horns. No one in New York had ever seen such an exciting show. They thought the Wild West Show was wonderful.

Bill visited many cities. Everywhere he went people cheered him.

"How does it feel to be the star performer of the rodeo?" Ted asked one afternoon. Bill smiled. "Aw—I'm no star. I just like bulldogging. Come on, let's go help load the animals."

Ted and Bill walked to the long line of railroad cars that belonged to the Wild West Show. The rodeo was getting ready to leave for another town.

"Six hundred animals in all," Bill said.
"It's no wonder we have to have so many
railroad cars."
"It's kind of hard to believe we can all
travel together and so far," Ted said.
Bill let out a whistle. "Look at those
elephants. I never get tired of watching
them."
He was happy in the great Wild West
Show.

4

When the show traveled to Mexico City, some newspapers carried stories about Bill Pickett. They said the Mexican bull-fighters did not think Bill could keep his hands on the horns of one of their bulls for more than five minutes. Bill said he could and would hold onto one of the giant bulls. "Be careful," Colonel Zack said. He looked at the huge crowd. "These people sure don't want to see you win. They think their bullfighters are better than you." "I'll watch out," Bill said.

His heart pounded as he watched the great spotted bull shaking its head angrily.

"Come on, Spradley," he said as they rode into the arena.

The bull charged toward Bill. Quickly Spradley stepped out of the way. Then the bull rushed at Spradley, pushing its horns into the horse's hind legs. Spradley fell, and Bill grabbed the sharp horns.

For five minutes the bull flung Bill back
and forth, but he held on with all his
strength. The crowd was angry. They
wanted Bill to lose the fight. Some of the
people picked up bottles and threw them.
One bottle hit Bill, and he nearly let go of
the horns.

"I've got to hang on," Bill said to himself.
"Just a little longer."

When at last the time was up, Bill had three ribs broken, but he had proved that he could hold onto a Mexican bull. He limped over to his horse. There were tears in Bill's eyes as he looked at Spradley. "Can anybody help my Spradley?" he asked.

A little Mexican man stepped forward. "I can if someone will get me some red bananas."
In a few minutes the little man was handed the bananas. He mashed and spread them onto Spradley's legs. Bill could not believe that the bananas would help, but he thanked the man.

Every night Bill slept beside Spradley. He never left his little horse. Spradley always had a bed of clean hay and all the food he could eat.

"Look at you, Spradley," Bill said one morning as he watched his horse eat. "You're growing stronger."

"You sound surprised," Ted said. He stepped into Spradley's stall.

"I am," Bill told him. "I was so afraid my little horse would die."

"You are quite a man," Ted said. "Not even a Mexican bull can scare you, but you were afraid for Spradley."

After a while Spradley could run as well as he ever had. Bill later learned that the bananas probably helped Spradley because they had large amounts of Vitamin C and potassium in them. Vitamin C is good for healing wounds. Potassium helped to stop the bleeding. Bill never forgot the Mexican man with the red bananas.

5

The 101 Wild West Show went to
England. The English people loved the
rodeo, and great crowds came to see the
cowboys. One night the show was seen by
the King and Queen of England.
"Look!" the King cried. "Look at that man
throwing the steer!"
The King became so excited that he
clapped loudly, and kings did not often do
that. At the end of the show Bill shook
hands with the King and Queen.
"Good show," the King said.
"Thank you," Bill said.

He had never thought that one day he would be talking with the King of England. An English nobleman liked Bill so much that he invited him to eat at his castle. Ted was waiting for Bill when he returned from the dinner.

"Imagine that," Ted said, laughing. "You didn't take Spradley along!"

Bill laughed, too.

The show did not stay in England as long as was planned. World War I began, and the English government took over almost all of Colonel Zack's horses and cars. The Wild West Show folded its tents and went home to America.

Many years passed before Colonel Zack could put the show together again. It was like having to start all over. During that time the cowboys of the 101 Ranch stayed busy branding and herding cattle. Bill and his Spradley were always together. Bill was growing older, but he could still bulldog a steer as well as anyone.
Ted still worked at the ranch, too. But he did not ride much any more.

Bill often stayed with Spradley at night
and slept on the soft hay in his stall.
People could hear him talking to his horse.
"Remember the time in New York when
we chased that old steer into the crowd?"
Spradley neighed softly. Some people said
he could understand every word Bill said.
"We sure showed everyone how to catch a
steer, didn't we?"

The Wild West Show cowboys had their rodeos and circus acts once in a while, but times were not easy on the 101 Ranch. Colonel Zack became ill.

"I'll help cheer up Colonel Zack and rope some horses," Bill said.

"Better not, Bill," said Ted. "There are some real wild ones in the corral today."

"That has never stopped me," Bill answered.

But when Bill stepped into the corral, one of the horses reared and kicked. Bill was an old man and could not move quickly. The horse knocked him down.

Bill Pickett died from his injury. He was seventy-two years old.

People all over the world were saddened by Bill's death. He had been a real cowboy—a friendly and brave man who had brought excitement and joy to many. He would always be remembered. Colonel Zack wrote a poem about his old friend.

Like many men in the old-time West,
On any job he did his best.
He left a blank that is hard to fill
For there will never be another Bill.

Four lines of poetry above are from *The 101 Ranch*, by Ellsworth Collings and Alma Miller England. Copyright 1937, 1971 by the University of Oklahoma Press.

Sibyl Hancock, author of several books for young readers, enjoys writing about subjects that require careful research and investigation. A collector of old children's books and an amateur astronomer, Ms. Hancock lives in a suburb of Houston, Texas, with her husband and eight-year-old son, Kevin, and two Persian cats called Tubby and Prissy.

Lorinda Bryan Cauley, a graduate of the Rhode Island School of Design, has just begun a promising career of illustrating children's books. This talented young artist lives in Ohio with her husband, a teacher of painting and drawing at Ohio State University. Ms. Cauley is a talented cook and is also interested in sewing and needlepoint.